The MAILBOX®

The Education Center®

CROSS-CURRICULAR PRESCHOOL PRACTICE

Preschool

W9-DBL-661

SUPER SIMPLE!

144 EASY-TO-USE IDEAS FOR SKILL REINFORCEMENT

- ☑ Beginning sounds
- ☑ Letters
- ☑ Art
- ☑ Fine motor

- ☑ Patterns
- ☑ Numbers
- ☑ Sorting
- ☑ AND LOTS MORE!

ENOUGH FOR
4 centers for every week
OF THE SCHOOL YEAR

Managing Editor: Kimberly Brugger-Murphy

Editorial Team: Lisa Addington, Becky S. Andrews, Kelly Ash, Randi Austin, Diane Badden, Deborah Baker, Dianne Baker, Janet Boyce, Tricia Brown, Kimberley Bruck, Karen A. Brudnak, Kitty Campbell, LeeAnn Collins, Camille Cooper, Mary Davis, Lynette Dickerson, Shanda Fitte, Carrie Flugel, Sarah Foreman, Michelle Freed, Sara Gales, Devorah Gongola, Tazmen Hansen, Marsha Heim, Lori Z. Henry, Colleen Higgins, Brenda Horn, Sharon Jenkins, Colleen Jones, Bonnie Lanterman, Donna Leonard, Debra Liverman, April Malaney, Dorothy C. McKinney, Thad H. McLaurin, Sarah Menck, Heather Miller, Brenda Miner, Sharon Murphy, Jennifer Nunn, Keely Peasner, Mary F. Philip, Mark Rainey, Sue Reppert, Greg D. Rieves, Jennifer Ritchie, Tara Robinson, Mary Robles, Leah Roddey, Hope Rodgers, Deborah Ryan, Eliseo De Jesus Santos II, Andrea Singleton, Barry Slate, Lisa Stewart, Donna K. Teal, Joshua Thomas, Christine Vohs, Paulette Vuchko, Carole Watkins, Zane Williard, Joyce Wilson

www.themailbox.com

Manufactured in the United States
10 9 8 7 6 5 4 3 2 1

Table of Contents

To use the table of contents as a checklist, make a copy of pages 2 and 3. Staple or clip each copy on top of its original page. Each time you use an activity, check its box. Start each school year with fresh copies of the pages.

Skills Index on pages 111–112.

Truck Full of Shapes

Math center: shapes

Materials:
poster board with block tracings as shown
blocks

A child places each block on the corresponding tracing. For added appeal, draw a colorful flatbed truck on the poster board.

Bubble Wrap Prints

Water table: artistic expression

Materials:
bubble wrap, taped inside an empty water table
tempera paint
paintbrush
paper

A child paints a picture on the bubble wrap. She places the paper on the bubble wrap and then smoothes the surface of the paper to transfer the picture. Finally, she removes her paper to view the finished print.

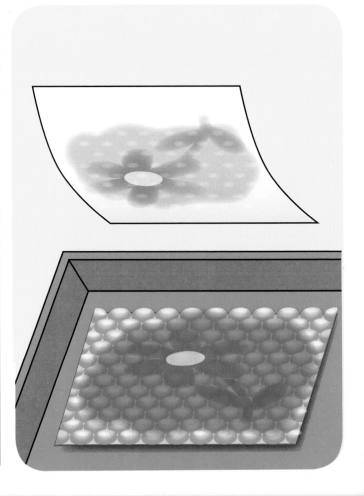

Alpha Blocks

Literacy center: letter exploration

Materials:
interlocking blocks labeled with letters

A student explores the blocks. She builds with the blocks or sorts them as desired. For an added challenge, the child places the blocks in alphabetical order.

Lots of Lids

Fine-motor area: size differentiation

Materials:
lidded containers in a variety of sizes

A youngster investigates the different sizes and shapes of the containers. Then she attaches each lid to its corresponding container.

Fun Goop

Science center: sense of touch

Materials:
mixture of cornstarch and water
utensils and measuring cups

A student uses his fingers to explore the unique texture of the mixture. If a child is hesitant to touch the mixture, he uses the utensils and measuring cups to investigate.

Which Box?

Math center: color identification

Materials:
3 boxes, each painted a different color
items in colors that match and that fit inside the boxes

A youngster chooses an item and identifies the color. Then she places the item in the matching box. She continues in the same way with the remaining items.

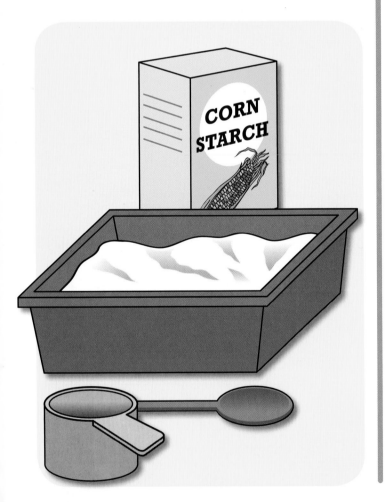

At the Zoo

Block center: pretend play

Materials:
copy of page 76, colored and attached
    to a wall near the center
blocks
plush or plastic zoo animals
paper
crayons
animal-related books (optional)

At this zoo-themed center, a youngster uses the blocks to build enclosures for the animals. He makes signs for the enclosures with the paper and crayons. If desired, he looks through the books to find photographs of the animals in his zoo.

Play Dough Letters

Fine-motor area: letter formation

Materials:
laminated sheets of tagboard labeled with letters
play dough

A student chooses a letter. Then she rolls the play dough into long ropes and places the ropes over the letter. She easily removes the play dough from the laminated surface.

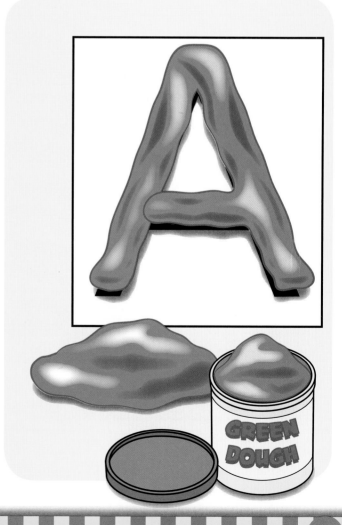

Tinted Ice

Water table: colors

Materials:
ice cubes made from water tinted two
    different primary colors, placed in
    a water table
mixing spoons

A student observes the ice cubes, noticing
how the colors blend together to tint the water
in the water table. She uses a spoon to gently stir
the water as she observes.

Picture Patterns

Literacy center: rhyming

Materials:
sentence strips prepared with rhyming
    AB patterns (cards on pages 80–81)
additional copies of the cards

A child chooses a sentence strip and reads the
pattern aloud to hear the rhyming words. Then
he places the matching cards below the sentence
strip to duplicate the pattern. He reads his pattern
aloud. Then the youngster repeats the process
with a new sentence strip.

Row of Rice

Math center: ordering by volume

Materials:
5 plastic bottles filled with varying amounts
    of colored rice (caps hot-glued to bottles)

A child observes the different amounts of rice
in the bottles; then she arranges the bottles in a
row from the one with the least amount of rice
to the one with the most rice. For an extra challenge, she rearranges the bottles from the one
with the most rice to the one with the least rice.

Blending Colors

Art center: artistic expression

Materials:
liquid laundry starch, slightly diluted
watercolors
paintbrush
white construction paper

A student brushes a layer of the liquid laundry
starch over the paper. Then she brushes stripes
of watercolors over the starch and watches as the
colors blend.

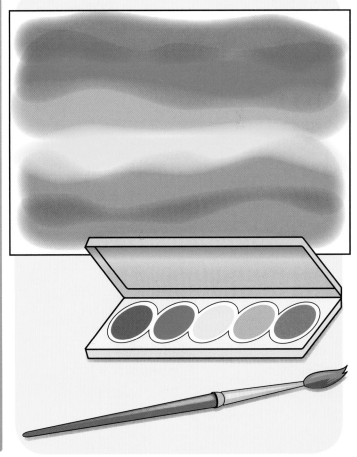

Sticker Story

Literacy center: writing

Materials:
stickers
blank paper

A youngster chooses stickers and places them on the paper as desired. Then she tells an adult a story about the images as the adult writes her story on the paper.

The dog is trying to catch the butterflies. He can't catch them. They fly really fast.

Cookie Cutter Combos

Fine-motor area: patterning

Materials:
cookie cutters
laminated sentence strips with patterns
    of cookie cutter tracings
play dough

A child chooses a sentence strip and the coordinating cookie cutters. He uses the cookie cutters to make several play dough cutouts; then he places the cutouts over the shapes on the sentence strip. Finally, the child reads the pattern.

Picture Day

Dramatic play: role-playing

Materials:
copies of page 77 attached to a clipboard
bulletin board paper attached to a wall as a backdrop
play camera
dress-up clothing and accessories
crayons

Youngsters pretend it's picture day as they sign their names to the clipboard and put on dress-up clothes. Then they pretend to take photographs of each other in front of the backdrop.

Boxes and Beyond

Block center: spatial skills

Materials:
boxes in a variety of sizes, taped closed
sponges
blocks of foam

A child visits the center and builds unique structures combining the regular blocks with the new items.

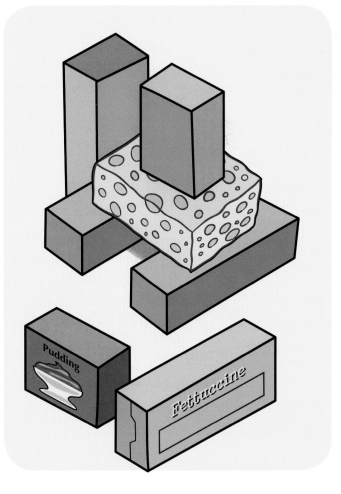

Beanbag Toss

Gross-motor area: throwing

Materials:
2 plastic hoops placed several feet apart
beanbags

A student takes a beanbag from the pile. He stands in one plastic hoop and tosses the beanbag into the other hoop. He continues in the same manner with the remaining beanbags.

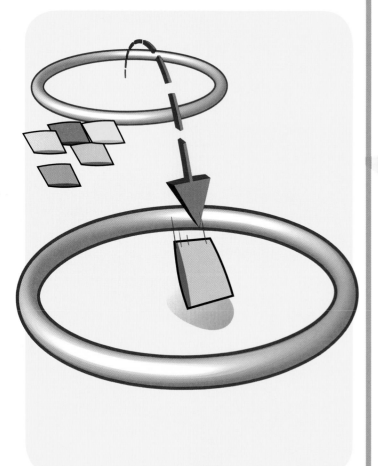

Elevation Station

Science center: prediction

Materials:
long, smooth board with one end elevated
several items, each a different weight, shape, and material

A youngster chooses an item and describes it. Then she predicts what will happen to the item when she places it on the elevated end of the board. She puts the item on the board and observes what happens.

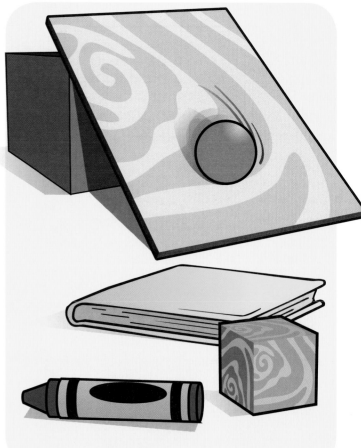

Letter Lacing

Fine-motor area: beginning sounds

Materials:
letter lacing cutouts with yarn attached as shown

    A child chooses a letter. He puts the loose end of the yarn through the hole closest to the attached end of the yarn. Then he makes the letter's sound as he pulls the yarn through the hole. He continues in the same manner until the lacing is complete.

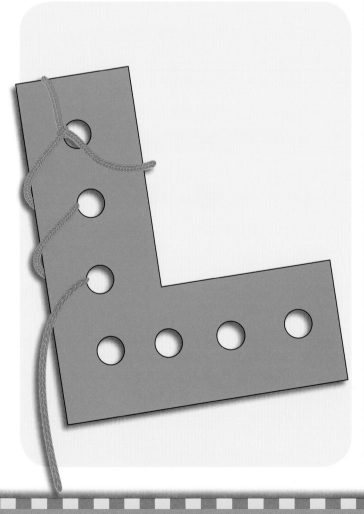

Coordinating Clothes

Math center: matching colors

Materials:
clothesline suspended between two chairs
spring-style clothespins
copy of pages 78 and 79, colored to make coordinating pairs and cut out

    A student selects a clothing cutout. Then she finds a different cutout of the same color. She uses a clothespin to clip the matching clothes on the clothesline.

Parking Garage

Literacy center: matching letters

Materials:
boxes (garages), each labeled with a different letter
toy cars, programmed with letters that correspond
  to the garages

A youngster chooses a car and "drives" it by
the garages. When he finds the garage with the
corresponding letter, he parks his car inside. He
continues in the same way with each car.

Searching the Sand

Sand table: counting

Materials:
number cards programmed with corresponding
  dot sets
objects to count, hidden in a sand table

A child picks a card and counts aloud the
number of dots on the card. She searches for
the corresponding number of objects hidden
in the sand. Then she counts aloud the number
of objects to confirm that she has the correct
number.

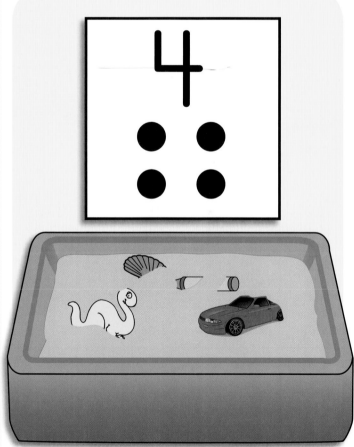

Dandy Dots

Art center: fine-motor skills

Materials:
cotton swabs
bingo daubers
construction paper
construction paper scraps
shallow containers of paint
hole puncher
glue

To make a dot picture, a student dips cotton swabs in the paint and then presses the swabs on a sheet of construction paper. She punches holes in the construction paper scraps and then glues the hole-punched dots to the paper. Then she adds larger dots with colorful bingo daubers.

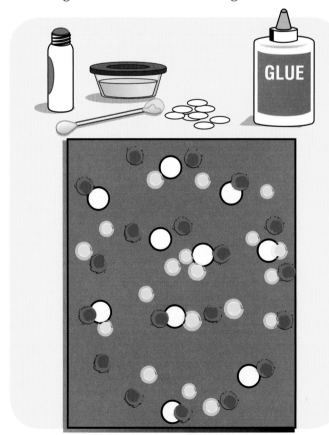

Sniff and Search

Science center: sense of smell

Materials:
tagboard cards readied with spice samples
    and labeled
cups of corresponding spice samples, with the cup
    bottoms labeled to match the cards

A youngster smells the spice in one cup. Then he smells the spice on each tagboard card to find the matching smell. He checks the label on the bottom of the cup to confirm that he found the matching spice.

cinnamon

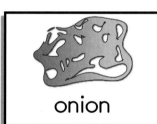

onion

oregano

garlic

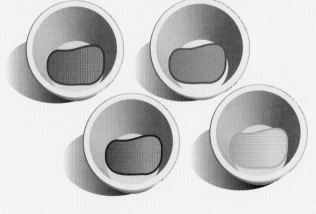

Picture Pairs

Literacy center: rhyming

Materials:
copy of the cards on pages 80 and 81, cut out and attached to blocks

A child chooses a block and names the picture on the card. She sorts through the blocks to find the corresponding card. Then she names the rhyming pair and sets the blocks aside.

Shape Clips

Math center: shape matching

Materials:
foam shapes hot-glued to spring-style clothespins
poster board circle programmed with matching shapes as shown

A student chooses a clothespin. He identifies the shape. Then he clips the clothespin to the section of the circle that has the matching shape. He continues in the same way with the remaining clothespins.

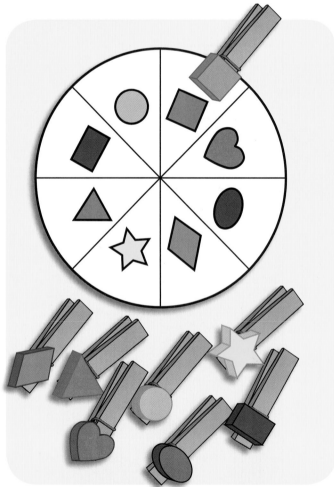

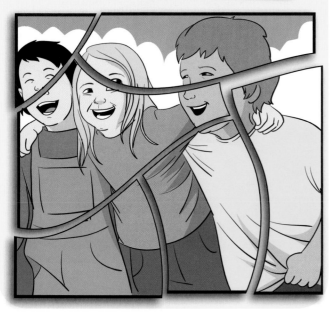

Photo Puzzle

Fine-motor area: spatial skills

Materials:
enlarged copy of a photograph, puzzle-cut and
   placed in an envelope
original photograph, attached to the envelope

A youngster removes the puzzle pieces from the envelope. She puts the puzzle together using the picture as a guide. Then she places the pieces back in the envelope.

Delicious Doughnuts

Dramatic play: role play

Materials:
baker's hat and apron
bakeware, utensils, and measuring cups
play dough
copy of page 82, colored and laminated

For this doughnut-making center, a child puts on the baker's hat and apron. He uses the bakeware, utensils, and play dough to act out making doughnuts that customers have ordered from the menu.

Woolly Sheep

Math center: number identification

Materials:
copies of the pattern on page 83, cut out and
    programmed with different numbers
cotton balls

    A student chooses a sheep and identifies
the number. Then she counts aloud the corresponding number of cotton balls and places them
on the sheep.

Zigzagging Around

Gross-motor area: various movements

Materials:
masking tape attached to the floor to show
    a meandering design

    A youngster walks along the length of the line.
He repeats the activity by crawling along the line
and then hopping along the line.

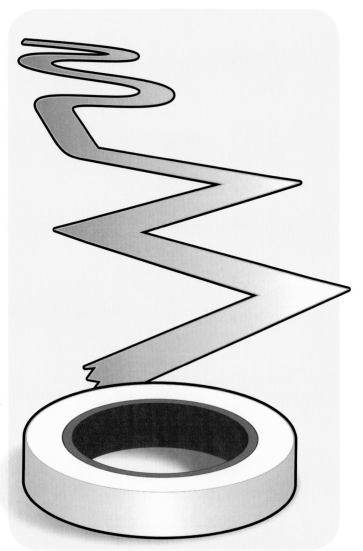

Bristle Designs

Art center: artistic expression

Materials:
clean brushes (hairbrush, bottle brush, toothbrush,
   scrub brush, paintbrush)
construction paper
shallow containers of paint

A child chooses a brush and dips the bristles in a container of paint. Then she paints on her paper with the bristles. She repeats the process with the remaining brushes to create a fun design.

Milk Cap Match

Literacy center: matching letters

Materials:
milk cap pairs labeled with matching letters
colorful copies of page 84, cut in half

A student chooses a car. Then he picks a milk cap and places it on a wheel. He looks for the milk cap with the matching letter and places it on the remaining wheel.

Finger Writing

Fine-motor area: writing

Materials:
large resealable plastic bag filled with
   a mixture of paint and white glue
tape

   Reinforce the bag with tape; then tape the bag to a tabletop. A youngster moves his finger across the bag to make letters, numbers, and pictures.

Community Workers

Math center: sorting

Materials:
copy of page 85, cut out and placed
   in different plastic hoops
chef, construction worker, and doctor props

   A child chooses a prop, identifies the community worker who may use it, and places it in the corresponding plastic hoop. She repeats the process for each remaining prop.

So Many Signs

Block center: pretend play

Materials:
copy of page 86, cards cut out and
    attached to blocks
road maps
masking tape placed on the floor so it resembles roads
building blocks
small toy cars and trucks

A child places the road signs near the masking tape roads. Then she uses blocks to make buildings for the town, consulting the map as desired. Finally, she "drives" the cars and trucks around the town.

Fancy Tissue

Art center: artistic expression

Materials:
facial tissues
containers of tinted water
eyedroppers
white construction paper (one per child)
diluted white glue
paintbrush

A youngster brushes diluted white glue over the construction paper. Then he tears pieces of facial tissue and places them on the glue. After the glue dries, he uses the eyedroppers to drip tinted water over the facial tissue pieces, observing the effect as the colors spread throughout the tissues.

Nifty Noodles

Math center: shapes

Materials:
shape cards, laminated for durability
cooked spaghetti noodles

A student chooses a shape card. She places noodles over the outline of the shape and then identifies the name of the shape. After she removes the noodles, she chooses a new shape card and repeats the process.

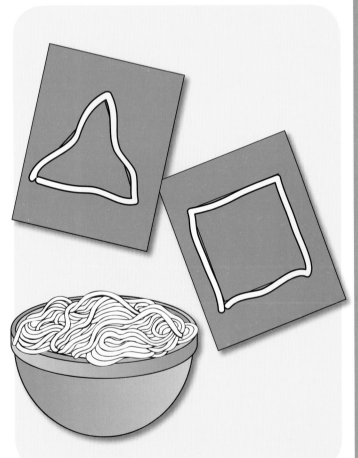

Where's the Top?

Literacy center: book awareness

Materials:
spring-style clothespins
picture books

A youngster visits the center and chooses a book. Then, after studying the book briefly, he attaches a clothespin to the top of the book. He repeats the process for each remaining book. (After youngsters can successfully identify the top of the book, you may want to repeat this center, having students clip the clothespin to the bottom or spine of the book.)

Library Day

Dramatic play: role-playing

Materials:
date stamp
picture books
writing paper
crayons

At this library-themed dramatic-play center, a child uses the items to role-play being a librarian or a patron at the library.

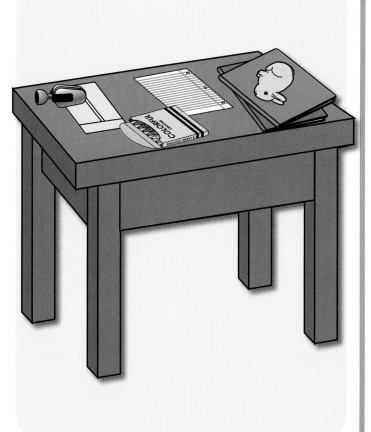

Alike and Different

Science center: observation skills

Materials:
tagboard, labeled as shown
resealable plastic bags of manipulatives (make sure that, in each bag, all the manipulatives are the same except for one)

A student opens a plastic bag and removes the contents. Then he places the manipulatives on the prepared tagboard, putting the manipulative that is different in the circle. When he's finished, he places the manipulatives back in the bag and then continues in the same way with a different bag.

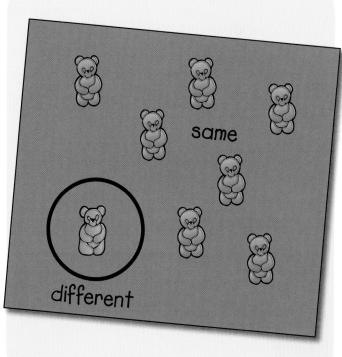

Cut 'n' Glue

Fine-motor area: fine-motor skills

Materials:
construction paper scraps
glue sticks
scissors (with both regular and fancy cuts)

Place all the items in a large tub or your empty water table. A youngster cuts the paper as desired and glues it to other pieces of paper until a desired effect is achieved.

Where's the Cheese?

Gross-motor area: counting

Materials:
10 pieces of yellow sponge (cheese),
    hidden around the classroom
length of crepe paper for each child
tape

For this mouse-themed center, a child tapes a length of crepe paper to his back so it resembles a tail. Then he searches for the cheese, counting the pieces as he goes until he finds all ten.

Scoop and Match

Literacy center: letter matching

Materials:
cookie sheet with tracings of magnetic
    letters in permanent marker
magnetic letters, placed in a plastic bowl
mixing spoon

With this unique baking center, a child uses the mixing spoon to stir the magnetic letters. Then he scoops up a letter and places it on the cookie sheet over the matching tracing.

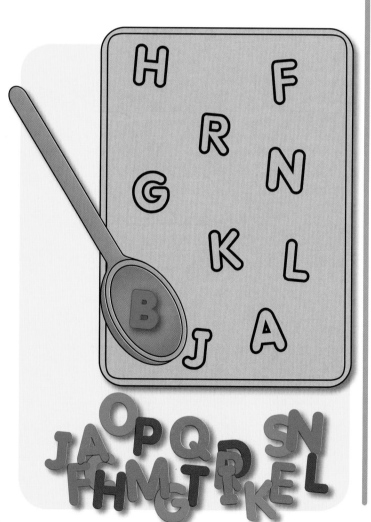

Flip and Rub

Art center: artistic expression

Materials:
stickers
masking tape
white construction paper
scissors (for cutting tape)
crayons with wrappers removed

A student places stickers and lengths of tape on a sheet of paper until a desired effect is achieved. Then she flips the paper over and rubs the crayons over the paper to the see the impressions of the items.

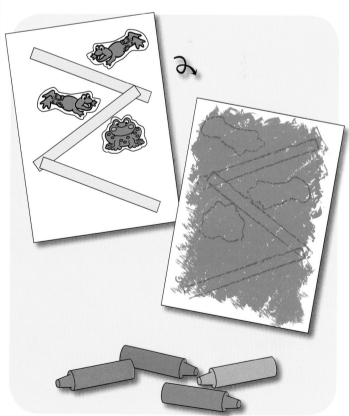

Shapely Frame

Water table: shape identification

Materials:
large acrylic picture frames
craft foam shape cutouts placed in a filled water table

A youngster chooses a shape floating in the water. Then she identifies the shape and places it on the acrylic frame. The moist shape clings to the frame!

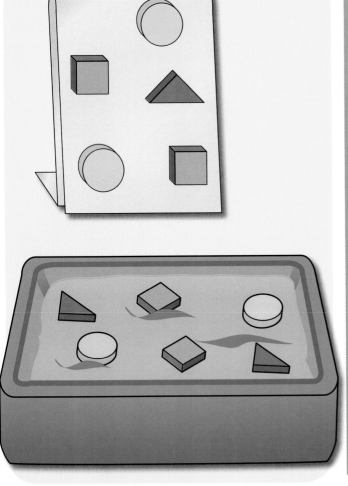

Photo Blocks

Block center: pretend play

Materials:
photographs of common buildings in
    your community, attached to blocks
additional building blocks
toy cars
people manipulatives

A youngster identifies the buildings in the photos. Then he uses those blocks and additional blocks to build a community. He moves the people and cars about the community, telling stories about them as he plays.

Terrific Letter *T*

Literacy center: beginning sounds

Materials:
copy of page 87, cut out
tooth cutout

A youngster chooses a card and says the name of the object pictured. If the name begins with /t/, she places the item on the tooth. If the name doesn't begin with /t/, she places the item in a separate pile.

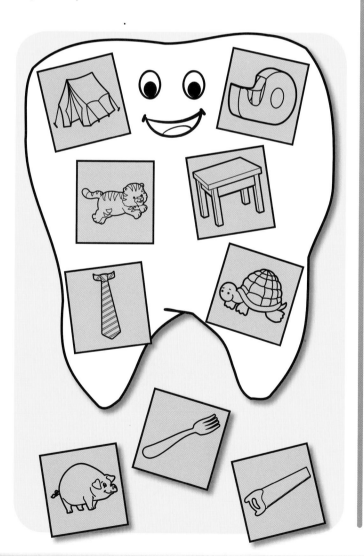

Busy Box

Science center: sense of sight

Materials:
cardboard box with a hole cut in the side
magazine pictures attached to the interior of the box
flashlight

A student shines the flashlight in the box and observes the pictures. Then the child discusses what she sees with a classmate or classroom helper. No doubt she'll see something new each time she looks in the box.

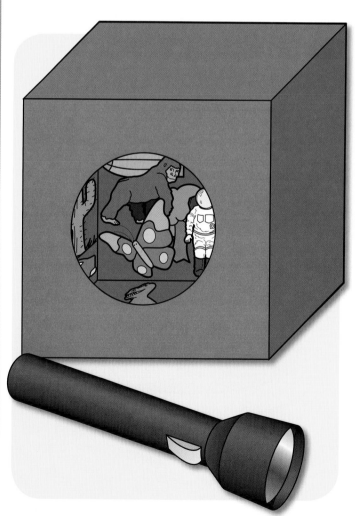

Gumballs Galore

Literacy center: rhyming

Materials:
enlarged copy of page 88 cut out
copy of page 89, colored and cut out

A student places all the gumballs on the gumball machine. He chooses a gumball and names the picture. Then he looks at the remaining gumballs to find a corresponding picture rhyme. He names the rhyming pair, removes the cards, and places them aside.

Fancy Foam

Math center: patterning

Materials:
strips of tagboard with patterns of
    self-adhesive foam shapes
supply of foam shapes to match the pattern strips

A youngster selects a pattern strip. Then she places a matching shape below the first shape in the pattern. She continues in the same manner with the remaining shapes until the pattern is complete.

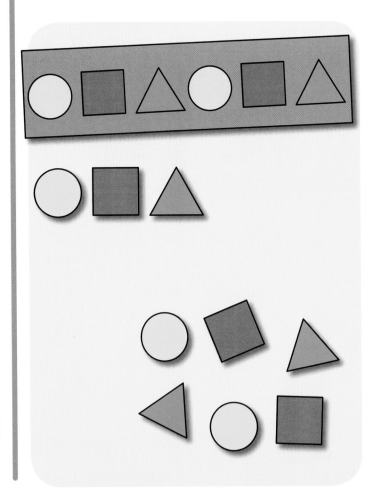

Pencil Painting

Art center: artistic expression

Materials:
paper (one sheet per child)
unsharpened pencils bundled together
    with a rubber band
shallow containers of paint

A child dips a bundle of pencils, eraser-side down, into a container of paint. Then he uses the pencils to make designs on his paper. He continues in the same way with the remaining bundles and paint until a desired effect is achieved.

Phone Number Puzzles

Fine-motor area: spatial skills

Materials:
telephone number puzzles placed in
    coordinating envelopes

A student removes the puzzle pieces from an envelope. Then she assembles the puzzle using the phone number on the envelope as a guide.

A Glorious Garden

Sand table: pretend play

Materials:
potting soil placed in the sand table
gardening props (plastic shovels,
 flowerpots, empty watering can,
 gloves, silk flowers)

At this gardening center, a youngster dons the gardening gloves and uses a shovel to fill a flower pot with soil. Then he chooses flowers and "plants" them by pushing the stems into the soil. He "waters" the flowers using the watering can.

Trace and Wipe

Literacy center: writing

Materials:
front panels from food boxes placed in
 resealable bags
baby wipes
washable markers

A child chooses a box panel. Writing on the bag, she uses a marker to trace each letter on the panel. Then she wipes the letters off the bag using a baby wipe.

Size Them Up

Math center: sorting

Materials:
copy of page 90, each animal colored, cut
 out, and attached to a different box
3 additional copies of page 90, including a
 reduced and an enlarged copy, colored
 and cut out

A student sorts the animals into the boxes by
animal type. Then he removes the animals from
each box, in turn, and arranges them in a row by
size.

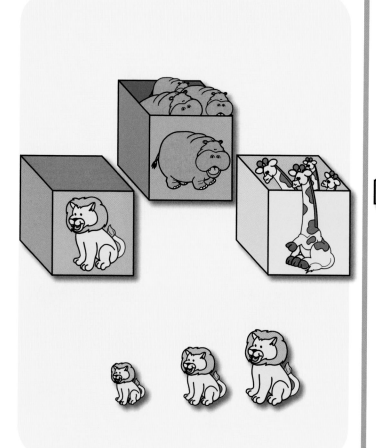

Dino Dig

Dramatic play: role-playing

Materials:
copy of page 91 displayed in the center
white shirts (paleontologists' lab coats)
craft foam bones buried in the sand table
small plastic shovels
dinosaur-related books
magnifying glasses
paintbrushes

At this dinosaur bone excavation center, a
youngster dons a lab coat and uses a shovel to
dig for bones. She uses a paintbrush to clean the
sand off the bones and then examines her discov-
eries using a magnifying glass. If desired, she
looks through the books to find pictures of prehis-
toric animals.

Peculiar Peacock

Literacy center: matching letters

Materials:
copy of page 92, colored, cut out, and attached
  to a tagboard circle labeled as shown
colorful spring-style clothespins, labeled as shown

A child chooses a clothespin. Then he clips
the clothespin to the circle next to the matching
letter. He continues in the same way with the
remaining clothespins.

How Many Blocks?

Block center: number identification

Materials:
5 number cards stored in a bag
blocks

A student picks a card from the bag and
identifies the number. Then she takes the corresponding number of blocks and uses them to
build a structure. She continues in the same
manner with the remaining cards.

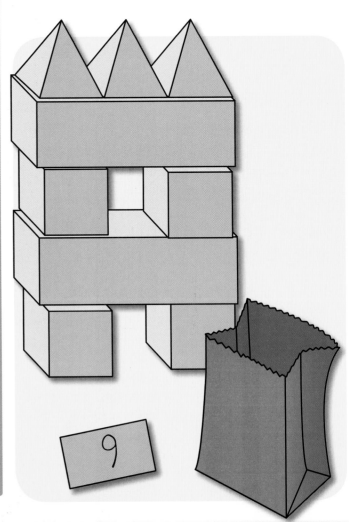

Rainbow Match

Math center: color sorting

Materials:
oversize rainbow cutout
items and pictures that match the rainbow's colors

A youngster chooses an item. Then he places the item on the corresponding arc of the rainbow. He repeats the process until all the items and pictures have been placed on the rainbow.

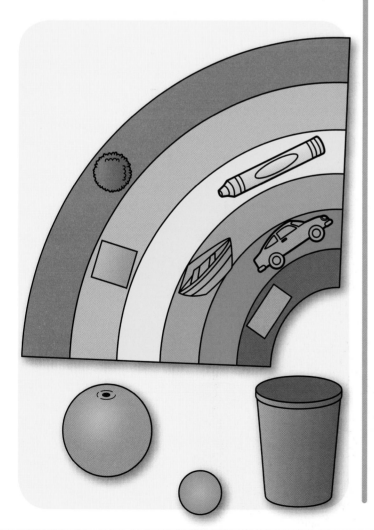

Mouse House

Fine-motor area: developing eye-hand coordination

Materials:
tissue box with the opening slightly enlarged (mouse hole)
spoon
large gray pom-pom (mouse)

A child places the mouse in a designated location a few feet from the mouse hole. The she uses the spoon to tap the mouse into the mouse hole.

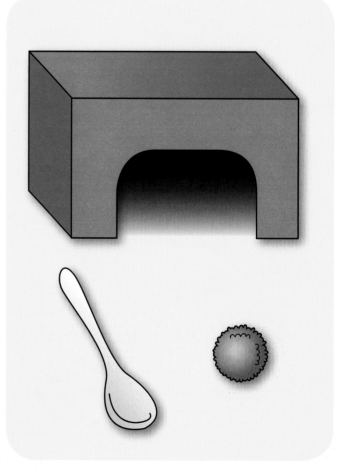

Pig in a Puddle

Literacy center: beginning sounds

Materials:
enlarged copy of page 93, colored and cut out
copy of page 94, colored and cut out

A student picks a card and names the picture. If the name of the pictured item begins with /p/, he places the card on the pig. If the name does not begin with /p/, he places the card to the side. He continues in the same manner with the remaining cards.

Shoe Sizes

Math center: ordering by size

Materials:
shoes in different sizes
bulletin board paper with tracings of the
    shoes in order from largest to smallest

A youngster compares the shoes in the pile to find the largest one. Then she places the shoe on the largest outline. She continues in the same way with the remaining shoes. For an added challenge, she lines the shoes up in order by size without using the shoe outlines as a guide.

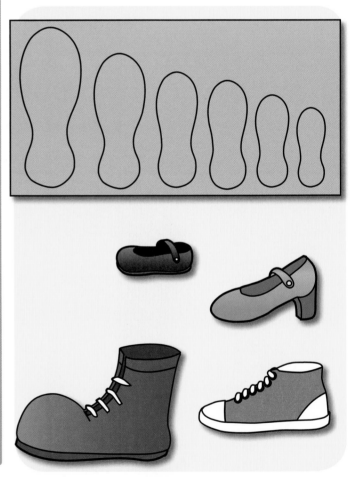

Textured Pairs

Science center: sense of touch

Materials:
pieces of textured material attached to poster board
matching pieces of material stored in a bag

A child feels the texture of a piece of material attached to the board. Then she reaches into the bag and feels the materials inside. She removes the piece of material that has the same texture and places it over the matching material on the board.

On a Roll

Art center: artistic expression

Materials:
objects that roll
large sheets of white paper (one per child)
shallow trays of paint

A student selects an object and rolls it in paint. Then he rolls the object across his paper. He repeats the process with the remaining objects until a desired effect is achieved.

What's in a Name?

Literacy center: letter identification

Materials:
letter tiles, arranged facedown
name card for each child

A youngster flips over a tile and identifies the letter. If the letter is in her name, she places it below the matching letter on her name card. If the letter is not in her name, she sets it aside. She continues in the same way until her name is complete.

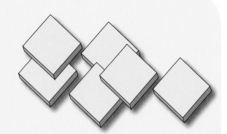

Fill 'er Up

Math center: measurement

Materials:
clear plastic bottles, labeled as shown
plastic pitcher filled with water
funnel

A child chooses a bottle and places a funnel in the opening. Then he uses the pitcher of water to fill the bottle to the programmed line. He repeats the process with each bottle; then he compares the amounts.

Going Buggy

Science center: living things

Materials:
copy of page 95, colored and cut out
bug cards (page 96), copied, colored, cut out,
   and hidden in the classroom

A student searches around the classroom to find a bug card. Then she brings the card to the center and places it on the Bug Collection Board over its matching picture. She repeats the process until she has found all the bugs.

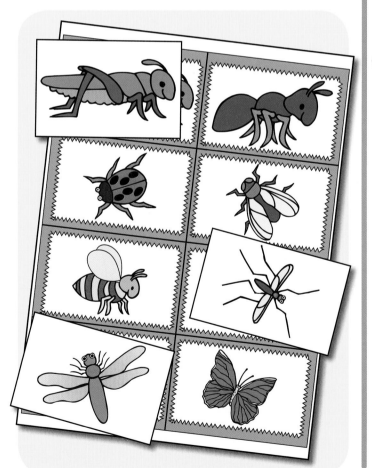

Excellent Exercise!

Gross-motor area: healthy habits

Materials:
copy of page 97, cut out and placed in a bag
floor mat
CD player with upbeat music (optional)

At this workout center, a youngster chooses a card from the bag and identifies the exercise. Then he does several repetitions of the chosen exercise. When he is finished, he sets the card aside and chooses a new card.

Rescue Hero

Dramatic play: role playing

Materials:
foam swimming pool noodle (fire hose)
fire safety props (hats, rubber boots,
    flashlights, first aid kit)

For this fire rescue–dramatic play activity, a child dons a firefighter's hat and boots. He uses the fire hose to put the fire out and then uses a flashlight to look for people who need help. Finally, he uses the first aid kit to take care of any injured people.

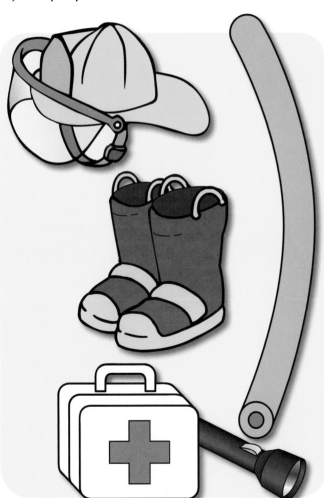

Overlapping Art

Art center: artistic expression

Materials:
objects that are easily traced (see below)
paper
black marker
crayons

A student places an object on the paper and then traces around the item with the marker. She places a different object on the paper overlapping the first tracing; then she traces around the item. She repeats the process until a desired effect is achieved. Then she uses the crayons to color the project.

Alphabet Munch

Literacy center: matching letters

Materials:
alphabet cereal
small alphabet chart for each child

A youngster gets a handful of cereal. Then he matches each piece of cereal to its corresponding letter on his chart. When he is finished matching all his letters, he eats the cereal.

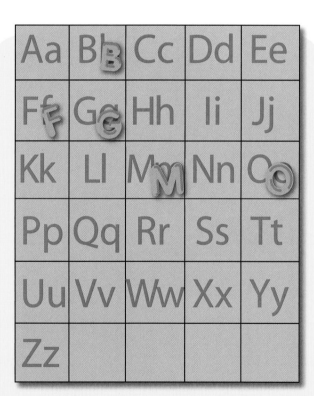

Rainbow Fish

Math center: sorting by color

Materials:
clear plastic cups, each labeled with a different-colored construction paper fish
pom-poms that match the color of each fish

A child sorts the pom-poms into the cups by color.

Shake and Build

Block center: sense of sound

Materials:
blocks
boxes with different items securely sealed inside

A student uses the blocks and boxes to build a structure. As he is building, he shakes the boxes to listen to the unique sounds.

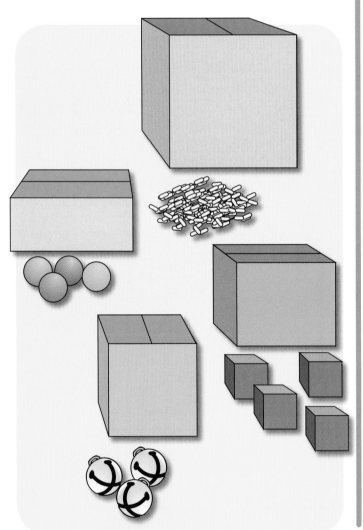

Clothespin Count

Math center: number identification

Materials:
tagboard cards, each labeled with a different number and its corresponding dot set
clothespins

A youngster chooses a card and identifies the number. Then she clips the corresponding number of clothespins to the card. She continues in the same manner with the remaining cards.

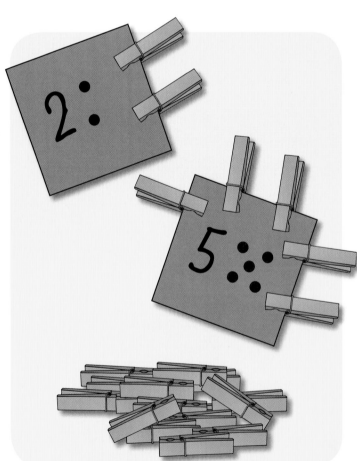

Time to Eat

Literacy center: beginning sounds

Materials:
box decorated so it resembles a bear
    with an open mouth
copy of page 98, cut out

A child picks a card and names the picture. If the name begins with /b/, he places the card in the bear's mouth. If the name does not begin with /b/, he sets the card aside. He repeats the process with the remaining cards.

Water Works

Fine-motor area: pincher grip

Materials:
water table filled with water
floating toys placed in the water table
spray bottles filled with water

A student aims the nozzle of a bottle at a floating toy. Then she pulls the trigger on the bottle to spray the target.

Driving Along

Math center: forming numbers

Materials:
oversize tagboard number cards, each
    labeled with a starting point (green
    dot) and stopping point (red dot)
small toy cars

A youngster chooses a number card and
places a car on the green dot. Then he "drives"
the car along the number, stopping when he
reaches the red dot. As he moves the car, he says
the name of the number.

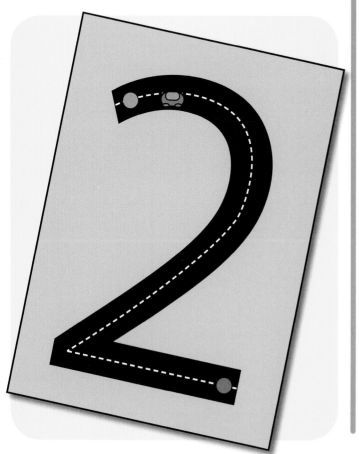

A Bone to Pick

Literacy center: rhyming

Materials:
dog bowl
copy of page 99, cut out

A child chooses a dog bone and names the
picture. Then she finds a dog bone with a picture
that rhymes with the picture on the first bone and
places the pair in the dog bowl. She continues in
the same way with the remaining dog bones.

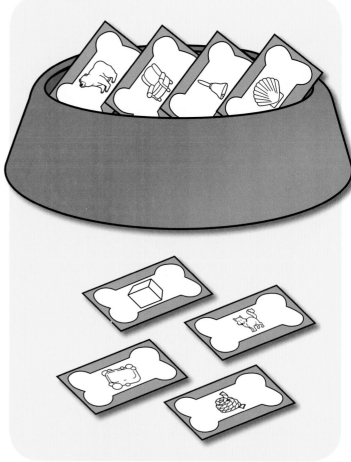

Swirl Art

Art center: artistic expression

Materials:
large fingerpaint paper
fingerpaint in several colors
plastic spoons
index cards, folded in half

A student uses the spoons to place dollops of paint on a sheet of fingerpaint paper. Then he uses an index card to spread the paint, swirling the colors together until a desired effect is achieved.

Office Work

Dramatic play: sorting by color

Materials:
small table (office desk)
file holder containing several different-colored folders
paper in colors that match the folders
stamp and ink pad

A youngster removes the folders from the file holder and places them on the desk. She takes a piece of paper and stamps it using the ink pad and stamp. Then she places the sheet of paper in the matching folder. She continues stamping, sorting, and filing the papers until her office work is done.

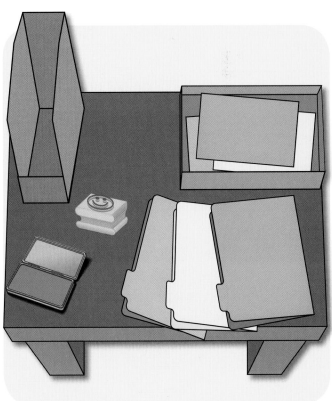

Worm Search

Science center: sense of touch

Materials:
sensory table filled with potting soil
plastic worms
plastic pail
blunt tweezers

A child uses his hands to dig through the potting soil to find worms. Then he pulls each worm out of the soil and places it in the pail. If the child is hesitant to touch the worms, he can pick them up using the tweezers.

Table Setting

Math center: number identification

Materials:
5 sheets of construction paper, labeled with outlines of dinnerware
5 each of plastic plates, cups, forks, knives, and spoons
number cards from 1 to 5

A student takes a card and identifies the number. Then she uses the placemats, plates, cups, and eating utensils to set the table with the corresponding number of place settings.

Newspaper Highlights

Literacy center: recognizing letters

Materials:
enlarged copies of several sections of a newspaper
sheet of tagboard labeled with a target letter
highlighters

A youngster chooses a newspaper section
and looks for an example of the target letter.
Then he uses a highlighter to highlight the letter.
He continues looking for the target letter, high-
lighting each one he finds.

Wiggly Snakes

Fine-motor area: stringing

Materials:
class supply of yarn lengths, each taped
    to a small cardboard tube section
additional cardboard tubes, cut into
    small sections and painted green
black marker
tape

A child chooses a length of yarn. She strings
additional tube pieces onto the yarn to create a
snake. With help, she tapes the loose end of the
yarn to the last tube section to secure it. Then she
uses the marker to draw features on her snake.

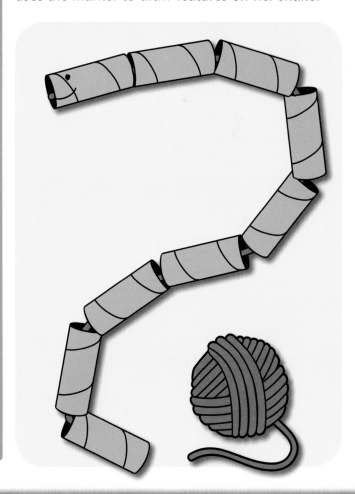

Tube Prints

Art center: artistic expression

Materials:
small cardboard tubes cut as shown
different colors of paint placed in a tray
    and swirled slightly
construction paper

A student chooses a tube and presses it in the paint. Then he presses the tube on his paper to make a print. He continues making prints until a desired effect is achieved.

Spotted Cow

Math center: counting

Materials:
enlarged copy of page 100, colored,
    cut out, and laminated
cow spot cutouts
large die

A youngster rolls the die and counts the dots. Then she counts aloud the corresponding number of spots and places them on the cow. She repeats the process several times until the cow is covered with many spots. Then she removes the spots and plays another round.

Gone Fishing

Water table: matching letters

Materials:
magnetic letters, placed in an empty water table
craft stick fishing poles with magnets
   tied on with string
alphabet chart

   A child uses a fishing pole to retrieve a letter from the water table. Then he places the letter on top of the matching letter on the alphabet chart.

Fabulous Felt

Fine-motor area: spatial skills

Materials:
felt in various colors, cut into small squares
simple pattern cards, similar to the one shown
blank card

   A student chooses a pattern card. Then she uses the felt squares to repeat the design on the blank card. She continues in the same manner with the remaining pattern cards.

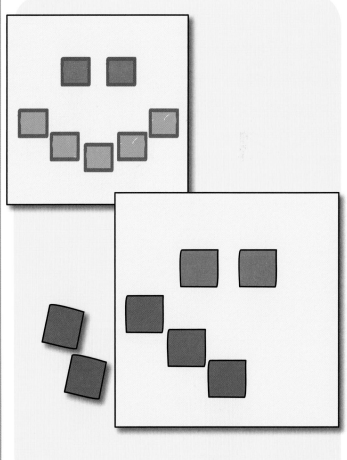

How Many Toothpicks?

Math center: measurement

Materials:
blunt toothpicks
common classroom items of different lengths

A youngster chooses an item. Then he places toothpicks next to the item to determine its length. When all the toothpicks are in place, he counts them. Then he removes the toothpicks and chooses a new item to measure.

Invisible Name

Literacy center: writing

Materials:
white paper
tinted water
cotton swabs
white crayon

A student uses the white crayon to write his name on his paper. Then he dips a cotton swab into the tinted water and paints the page. He repeats the process with the remaining colors until he reveals each letter in his name.

Hammer Time

Gross-motor area: pounding

Materials:
large wood block
plastic hammers
large die

A child rolls the die and counts the dots. Then she uses a hammer to pound on the wood the corresponding number of times.

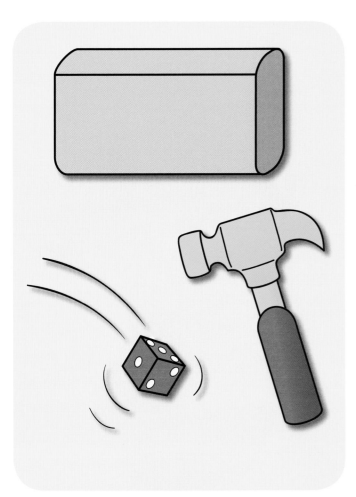

Pet Prescriptions

Dramatic play: role-playing

Materials:
student copies of page 101, attached to a clipboard
stuffed animals (sick pets)
medical props, such as a stethoscope and scale
white shirts (veterinarians' coats)
notepads

At this animal hospital center, a youngster dons a veterinarians' coat and uses the medical tools to treat a sick pet that has been signed in by its owner. Then she writes a prescription on the notepad. She continues in the same manner, treating other sick or injured animals.

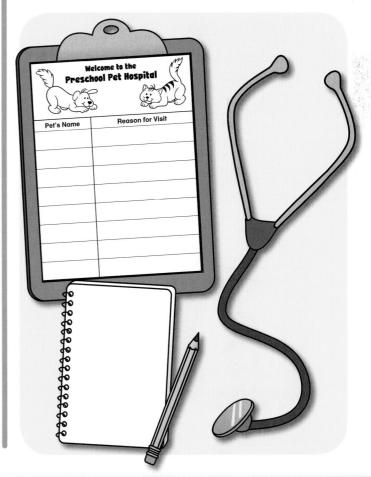

Searching for /s/

Sand table: beginning sounds

Materials:
sand table filled with sand
copy of pages 102 and 103, cut out, laminated,
    and placed in the sand table
plastic pail labeled as shown

A child digs through the sand to find a hidden card. Then he takes the card out of the sand and names the picture. If the picture begins with /s/ as in the word *sand,* he places the card in the pail. If it does not, he places the card to the side.

Alligator Chomp

Art center: following directions

Materials:
white construction paper triangles
pink construction paper tongue cutout (one per child)
paper plates, painted green (one per child)
glue
black marker

A student glues triangles (teeth) around the edge of the plate as shown; then he folds the plate in half. Next, he glues the tongue along the inside of the fold and uses the marker to draw facial details. Finally, he uses his hand to open and close the plate in a chomping motion.

Royal Crowns

Fine-motor area: squeezing

Materials:
enlarged laminated copies of page 104
several colors of play dough

A youngster chooses a crown. Then she molds and shapes pieces of play dough so they resemble jewels and places them on the crown.

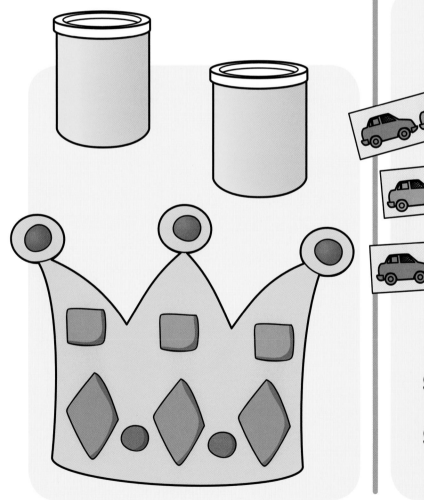

Cruising Cars

Math center: extending a pattern

Materials:
car patterning strips (car pattern on page 105)
additional car cutouts that match the cars on the strips

A child chooses a strip and reviews the pattern of cars. Then he finds the car that comes next in the pattern and places it after the final car on the strip. He continues to extend the pattern.

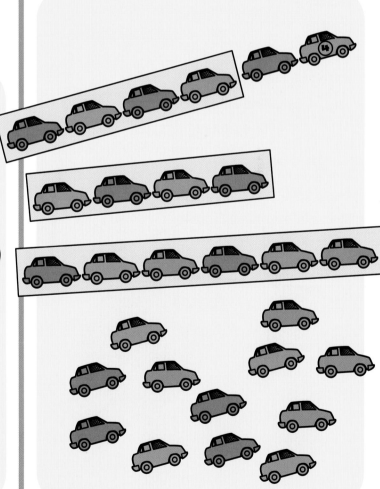

Havin' a Ball!

Gross-motor area: throwing

Materials:
soft foam balls
target, mounted on a wall

A student chooses a ball. She throws the ball at the target using an underhand throw. Then she throws the ball at the target using an overhand throw.

Plates of Pasta

Literacy center: matching letters

Materials:
alphabet pasta
paper plates, each labeled with a different letter

A youngster chooses a plate. Then he finds a matching pasta letter and places it on the plate. He continues in the same manner with the remaining plates.

Hidden Shapes

Science center: identifying shapes

Materials:
sensory table (or tub) filled with cornmeal
craft foam shapes hidden in the cornmeal
containers, each labeled with one
    of the matching shapes

A child digs through the cornmeal, pulls out a shape, and identifies it. Then she places the shape in the corresponding container. She continues in the same way with the remaining shapes.

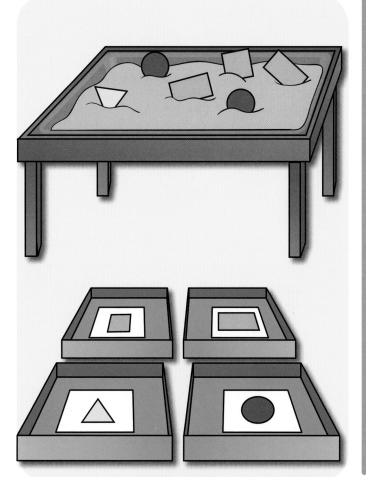

Pizza Party

Fine-motor area: imaginative play

Materials:
laminated brown construction paper
    circles (pizza crust)
play dough
rolling pins and plastic knives

A child uses a rolling pin to flatten a portion of red play dough so it resembles sauce. Then he places the flattened dough on the pizza crust. He shapes toppings from the remaining play dough and places them on the pizza.

Ready, Set, Go!

Science center: prediction

Materials:
board, positioned to make a ramp
several toy cars of different sizes and
    made of different materials

A youngster chooses two cars and predicts which one she thinks will roll to the bottom of the ramp first. Then she rolls the cars down the ramp and observes what happens. She compares her prediction to the outcome of the race.

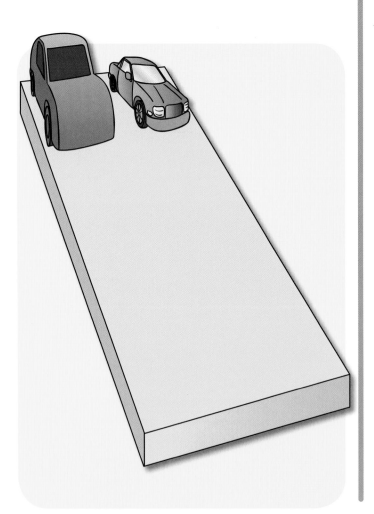

Make a Square

Fine-motor area: shapes

Materials:
2 identical poster board squares, one
    of which is cut into 4 triangles

A student spreads the triangles out on a surface. Then he arranges the triangles on top of the whole square to form the shape.

Lily Pad Pond

Math center: counting

Materials:
pond cutout
lily pad cutouts
supply of green pom-poms (frogs)
large die

A student rolls the die and counts aloud the number of dots. Then she counts aloud the corresponding number of frogs and places them on a lily pad. She continues in the same way with each remaining lily pad.

Copycat

Literacy center: matching letters

Materials:
tagboard cards, programmed as shown
plastic letters

A youngster chooses a card. Then he finds a matching letter and places it on the card. He continues placing matching letters on the card until the word is complete.

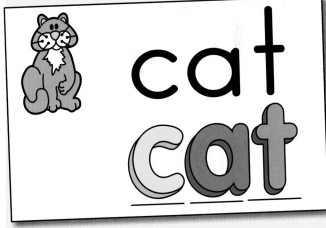

Pleasing Packing Pieces

Art center: artistic expression

Materials:
packing pieces
cardstock (one piece per child)
glue
tempera paint
paintbrushes

A child glues packing pieces to a sheet of cardstock to create a design. After the glue has dried, she paints the design as desired.

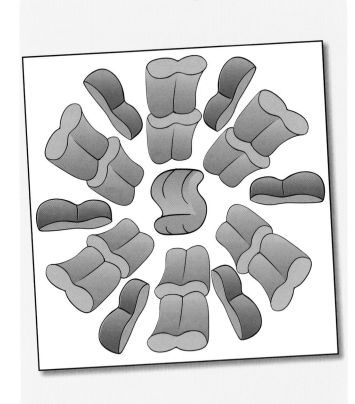

Roadblocks

Block center: letter formation

Materials:
blocks
sheets of poster board, each labeled with
    a letter and directional arrows
toy cars

A student selects a card and places blocks along the outline of the letter. Then he uses the arrows as a guide to drive a toy car along the letter. He repeats the process with the remaining letters.

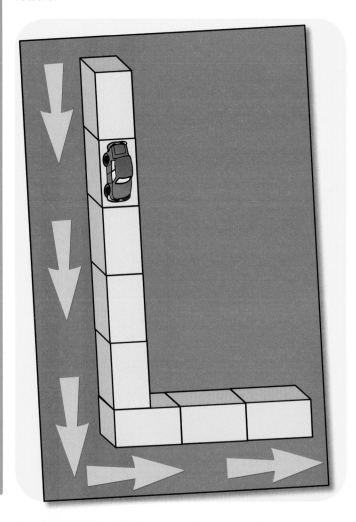

Special Delivery

Literacy center: writing

Materials:
name cards with photographs, stored in a bag
envelopes (one per child)
paper
markers

A student picks a name card from the bag. He uses it as a guide to write the classmate's name on an envelope. Next, he draws a picture on a sheet of paper, signs his name, and puts the paper in the envelope. Then he gives the envelope to the child.

Mail Carrier Math

Dramatic play: matching numbers

Materials:
blue button-up shirt and cap (mail carrier uniform)
3 boxes (mailboxes), each labeled with
    a different number
envelopes labeled with numbers that match
    the mailboxes and placed inside a tote
    bag (mailbag)

A youngster dons the mail carrier uniform and gathers the mailbag full of mail. Then she takes an envelope from the mailbag and places it in the mailbox with the matching number. She continues in the same manner with each remaining envelope.

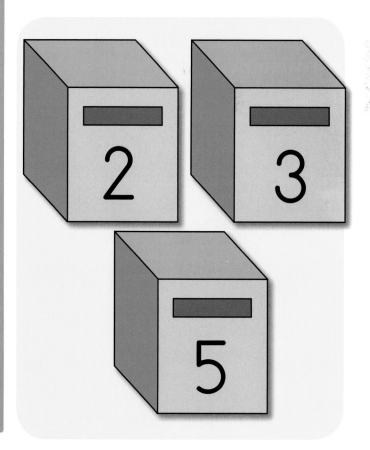

Move to the Beat

Gross-motor area: dancing

Materials:
CD player
compact discs of upbeat music
dance props, such as scarves, cheerleading
    pom-poms, and streamers

A child chooses a dance prop. He moves his prop with dramatic flair as he dances to the beat of each song.

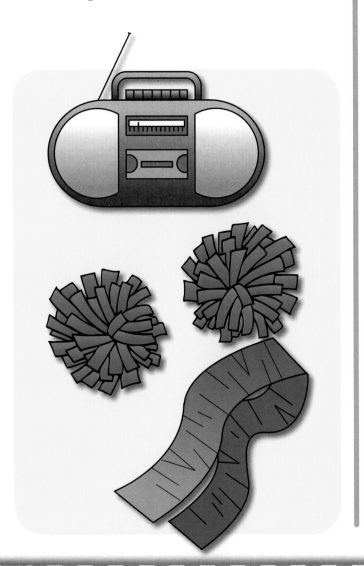

Repeat That, Please

Literacy: print awareness

Materials:
sentence strip pairs, each labeled
    with identical sentences
pocket chart

A student looks at a sentence strip that has been placed in the pocket chart. Then she finds the matching sentence and places it in the pocket chart below the sentence strip. She repeats the process with the remaining strips.

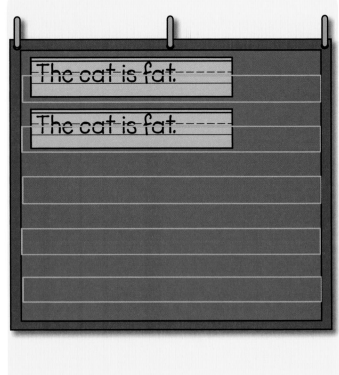

Play Dough Palette

Fine-motor area: matching colors

Materials:
poster board artist's palette with previously painted
   color blotches
play dough

A youngster selects a portion of play dough.
Then he places the play dough on the palette
over the matching paint. He continues in the
same way with the remaining play dough.

Creeping Caterpillar

Math center: ordering numbers

Materials:
11 green tagboard circles programmed as shown
number line labeled with numbers 1–10

A child places the circle labeled "1" beside
the caterpillar's head. Then she places each
remaining circle in the proper numerical order
to complete the caterpillar. If desired, she uses
the number line as a guide.

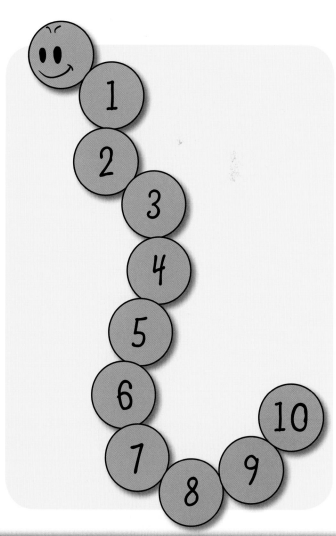

A Marvelous Mixture

Art center: artistic expression

Materials:
paper
shaving cream mixed with tempera paint
plastic spoons

A student uses a spoon to place a dollop of the mixture on his paper. Then he uses his fingers to draw a picture in the mixture. Next, he places a sheet of paper on top of his picture and gently smooths his hand across the paper. Finally, he lifts the paper and reveals the transferred picture.

Shopping Spree

Dramatic play: number identification

Materials:
grocery items labeled with numbers
    from 1 through 10
money bag filled with a supply of
    craft foam circles (coins)
cash register
grocery basket

In this grocery-shopping center, a youngster chooses an item, identifies the corresponding number, and places the item in her basket. Then she counts aloud the correct number of coins to pay for the item and gives the money to the grocery clerk.

Pick a Card

Math center: matching numbers

Materials:
playing cards (number cards only), stacked facedown
9 disposable cups labeled with numbers 2–10

A child draws a card from the stack. Then he places the card in the cup labeled with the matching number. He continues in the same manner with the remaining cards.

Swat That Fly!

Literacy center: rhyming

Materials:
copy of the cards on page 106, cut out
hard hat labeled "Exterminator"
shoebox labeled "Bug Box"
flyswatter

A student swats a card with the flyswatter and names the picture. Then she swats a second card and names the picture. If the pictures rhyme, she places the cards in the bug box.

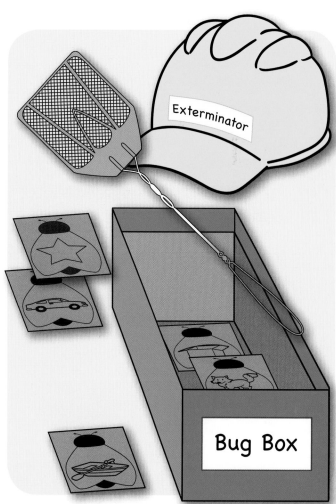

Hidden Treasures

Science center: sense of touch

Materials:
sensory table filled with dry oatmeal
small objects hidden in the oatmeal
plastic bowl
tongs

A youngster explores the texture of the oatmeal with his fingers as he searches for hidden objects. Then he removes each object from the oatmeal and places it in the bowl. If the youngster is hesitant to touch the oatmeal, he searches for the objects with the tongs.

A Pressing Project

Fine-motor area: artistic expression

Materials:
large pieces of floral foam or packing foam
colorful caps and lids, such as those
    found on milk or soda bottles

A child chooses a piece of foam and then presses lids and caps into the foam. When a desired effect is achieved, she displays her art for all to see.

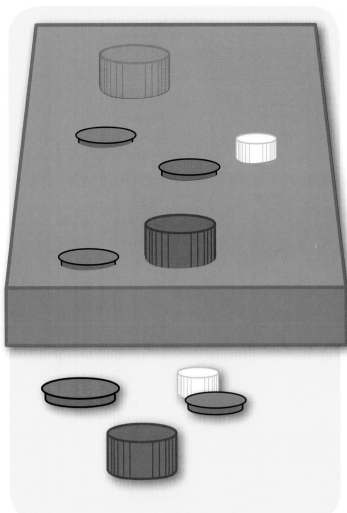

Storyteller

Literacy center: writing

Materials:
copy of the patterns on page 107; colored, cut out,
   and readied for flannelboard use
paper
flannelboard
marker

A student chooses a story piece and places it on the flannelboard. Then he begins to dictate a story to an adult helper. He adds story pieces to the board and continues dictating until his story is complete. Finally, the adult helper reads his dictation aloud.

There was a fox who lived in a house. One time, a girl came to visit the fox. She was very nice.

Silly Soup

Math center: number identification

Materials:
number cards
soup pot
wooden spoon
baskets of manipulatives

At this silly soup center, a youngster picks a card and identifies the number. Then she chooses a basket of manipulatives, counts aloud the corresponding number of items, and places them in the soup pot. She stirs the soup and then continues in the same way with the remaining cards and items.

Catalog Collage

Art center: artistic expression

Materials:
catalogs
scissors
paper
glue

A child looks through several catalogs and cuts out desired pictures. Then he glues the pictures to a sheet of paper to create a collage.

Building Bag

Block center: recognizing shapes

Materials:
blocks
tagboard cards with block tracings, stored in a bag

A student chooses a card from the bag. Then she finds the corresponding block and uses it to begin a structure. She continues in the same way with the remaining cards and blocks to complete her structure.

Spot the Dog

Literacy center: matching uppercase
and lowercase letters

Materials:
enlarged copy of page 108
spot cutouts labeled with individual
    uppercase and lowercase letters and
    sorted into separate containers

A youngster picks a spot from the uppercase
letter container and places it on the dog. Then he
finds the spot with the matching lowercase letter
and places it on the dog alongside the uppercase
letter. He continues in the same way with the
remaining spots.

Rainbow Stations

Math center: color identification

Materials:
rainbow outline for each child
crayons (each rainbow color placed at a separate
    station)

A child goes to the station with the red
crayons and identifies the color. Then he uses a
red crayon to color the outer arch of his rainbow.
He continues in the same manner, moving to
each color station in the correct order, until his
rainbow is complete.

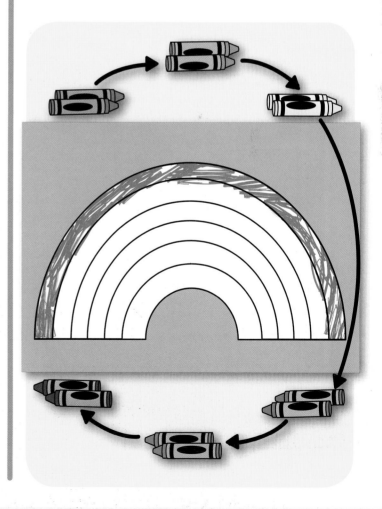

Small, Medium, Large

Math center: sorting by size

Materials:
3 boxes in different sizes, labeled as shown
small, medium, and large items

A student chooses an item. Then she decides whether the item is small, medium-size, or large in comparison to the other items. Then she places the item in the appropriate box. She continues in the same way with the remaining items.

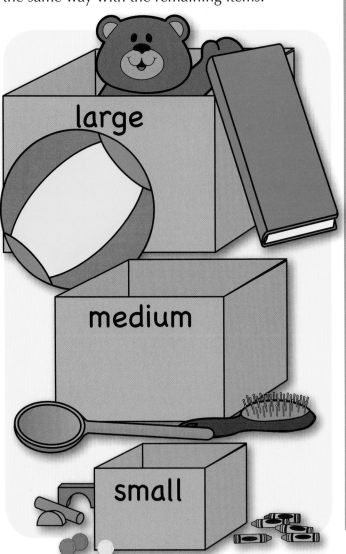

Count and Toss

Gross-motor area: number identification

Materials:
number cards
soft foam balls
laundry basket

A youngster chooses a card and identifies the number. Then he counts aloud the corresponding number of balls and tosses them one at a time into the laundry basket.

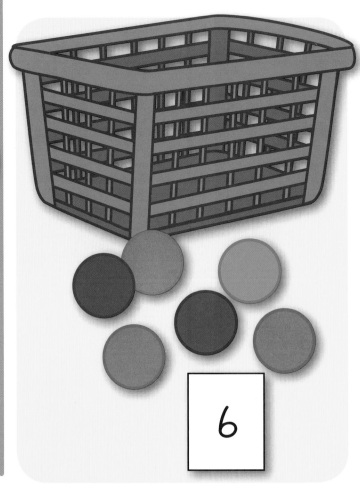

Letter Pie

Literacy center: letter identification

Materials:
letter cards
pie tin filled with play dough (pie)
magnetic letters

A child picks a card and identifies the letter. Then he finds a matching magnetic letter and presses it into the pie. He continues in the same way with each remaining card.

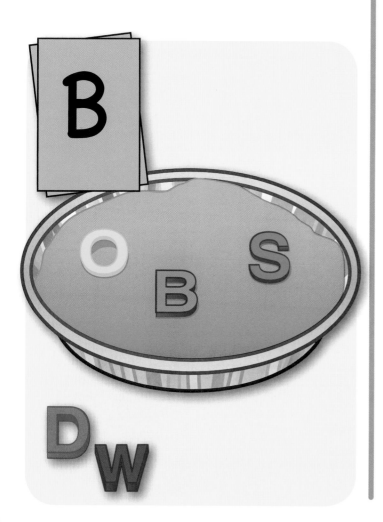

Preschool Express

Dramatic play: role-playing

Materials:
shirt and hat (conductor's uniform)
small table, labeled "Ticket Booth"
paper rectangles (train tickets)
play money
wallets and purses
chairs, lined up to create train seats

In this train station center, a student dons the conductor's uniform and sells tickets to customers. He calls out, "All aboard!" to the oncoming passengers and then collects the tickets that were purchased at the booth. Then he sits in the conductor's seat and says, "Choo, choo!" as he pretends to drive the train.

Brighter Colors

Science center: observation

Materials:
clear plastic cups containing equal
    amounts of food coloring
pitcher of water
coffee filters
paintbrushes

A youngster observes as unequal amounts of water are poured into each cup. Then he uses the mixtures to paint a coffee filter. With guidance, he notices that the food colorings with less water are brighter than those diluted with a large amount of water.

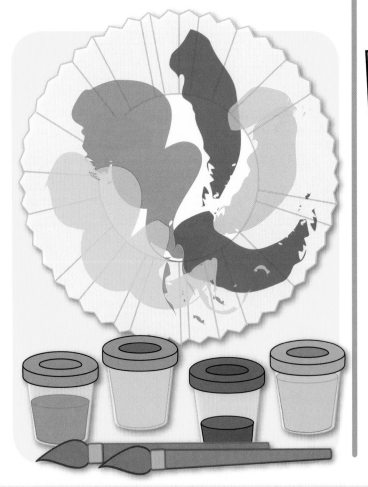

Oodles of Noodles

Math center: graphing

Materials:
small cup of tinted dry macaroni
    in four different colors
graph similar to the one shown

A child sorts each noodle onto its corresponding column. Then she looks at the graph and compares the columns.

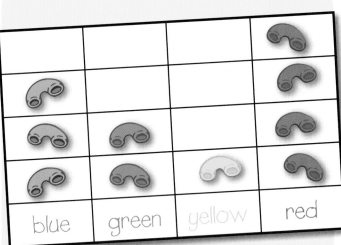

blue	green	yellow	red

Mounds of Rice

Sensory center: letter identification

Materials:
sensory table filled with dry rice and plastic letters
plastic container

A student uses his hands to dig through the rice to find a hidden letter. Then he pulls the letter out of the rice, identifies it, and places it in the container. He continues in the same manner with the remaining letters.

Giant Postcard

Literacy center: writing

Materials:
poster board, programmed with lines and laminated
name and address card for each child,
    placed in a file box
wipe-off markers
spray bottle filled with water
paper towels

A youngster removes her card from the file box and uses it as a guide to write her name and address on the poster board (postcard). Then she sprays the postcard with water and uses a paper towel to remove the writing.

Big Blueberry Muffin

Fine-motor area: counting

Materials:
brown construction paper copies of
    page 109, cut out
plastic bowl filled with small blue
    pom-poms (blueberries)
large die

A child rolls the die and counts aloud the number of dots. Then he counts aloud the corresponding number of blueberries and places them on the muffin. He removes the blueberries, places them back in the bowl, and continues in the same manner as before.

Boxes of Food

Math center: sorting

Materials:
empty food boxes from breakfast foods,
    dinner foods, desserts, and snacks

A student sorts the food boxes into the categories mentioned above. Then she sorts the boxes again according to what she likes to eat and what she doesn't like to eat.

Leafy Letter Tree

Literacy center: letter identification

Materials:
tree cutout, attached to a wall
die-cut leaves, each labeled with a letter
Sticky-Tac

A youngster takes a leaf and identifies the letter. Then he uses Sticky-Tac to attach the leaf to the tree. He continues in the same way with the remaining leaves.

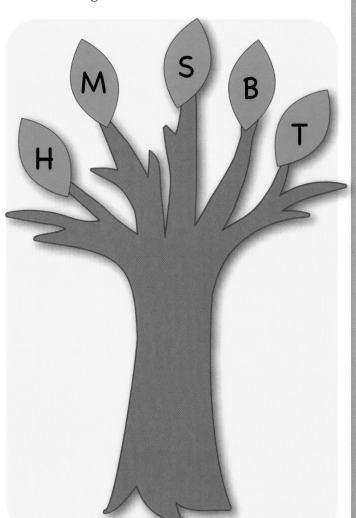

Where Are the Animals?

Block center: positional words

Materials:
blocks
plastic farm animals

A child uses the blocks to build an enclosed fence for the animals. She places the animals in several locations, such as inside, behind, in front of, beside, and on top of the fence. Then she uses the positional words to identify the location of each animal.

Make a Match

Science center: sense of touch

Materials:
common household items, stored in a pillowcase
photographs of the items

A student chooses a photograph and names the item. Then he reaches into the pillowcase and uses his hands to feel for the matching item. He pulls the item out of the pillowcase and places it to the side with the photograph.

Absorbing Water

Science center: prediction

Materials:
items that will and will not absorb water
plastic bowl with water
eyedroppers
chart similar to the one shown, laminated

A youngster selects an item and predicts whether she thinks the item will absorb water. Then she uses an eyedropper to drip several drops of water on the item. After observing the outcome, she places the item on the corresponding column on the chart.

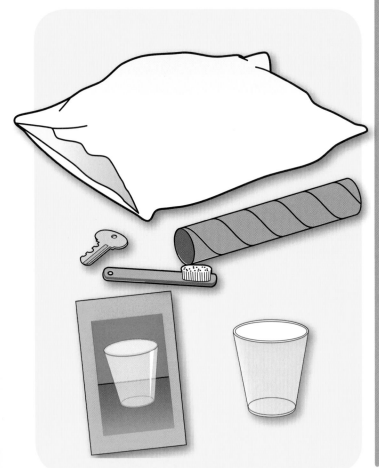

Absorbs Water	Does Not Absorb Water

Fabulous Flower Shop

Dramatic play: role playing

Materials:
flower shop props (flowerpots, artificial
    flowers, floral foam, watering cans,
    and gardening gloves)
play phone
notepads
markers
flower-related books and magazines

In this flower shop center, a child speaks to a
customer on the phone and then uses a notepad
and a marker to write down the order. Then
he dons his gardening gloves, puts a piece of
floral foam in a flowerpot, and makes a flower
arrangement. If desired, he uses the books and
magazines for inspiration for making flower
arrangements.

Shorter or Longer?

Math center: measurement

Materials:
jumbo craft sticks
supply of common objects

A student selects an object and compares its
length to the length of the craft stick. He decides
whether the object is shorter than, longer than,
or the same length as a craft stick. He repeats the
process with the remaining objects.

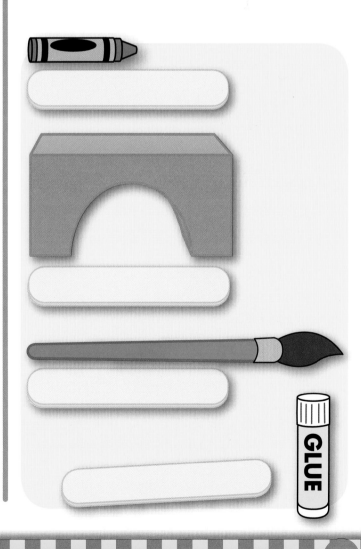

Flower Power

Art center: artistic expression

Materials:
artificial flowers
vase cutouts (one per child)
sheets of construction paper (one per child)
green crayons
shallow pans of tempera paint
glue

A youngster selects a vase and glues it to a sheet of paper. Next, he uses a green crayon to draw stems and leaves. Then he dips a flower in paint and presses it above a stem to make a print. He continues in the same way to make a beautiful bouquet of flowers.

Chain Links

Fine-motor area: number identification

Materials:
sheet of tagboard, labeled with a number
    and attached to a wall
construction paper strips
glue stick
tape

A child identifies the number. Then she uses the paper strips and glue to make a chain with the corresponding number of links. She tapes her finished chain to the tagboard.

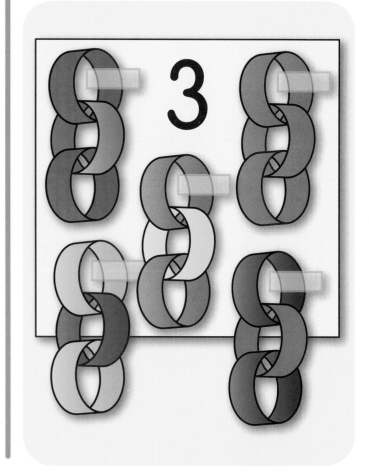

Supersize Cell Phone

Math center: number formation

Materials:
poster-size copy of page 110, cut out and laminated
name and phone number card for each
    child, placed in a file box
wipe-off markers
spray bottle with water
paper towels

    A student removes his card from the file box and uses it as a guide to write his phone number in the window of the cell phone cutout. Then he sprays the phone with water and uses a paper towel to remove the writing.

Alphabet Line

Literacy center: ordering

Materials:
length of clothesline, attached to a wall
clothespins
alphabet strip
alphabet cards

    A youngster finds the letter *A* card and uses a clothespin to clip it to the left side of the clothesline. She continues in the same way, clipping the remaining cards to the clothesline in order. If needed, she looks at the alphabet strip and sings the alphabet song to help guide her.

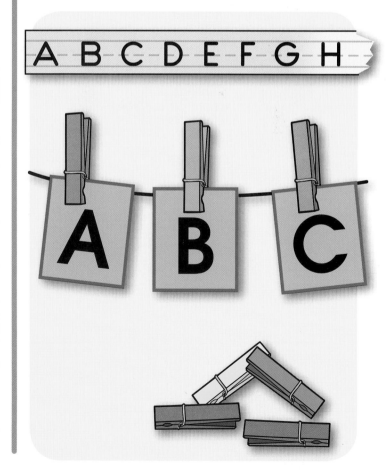

WELCOME TO THE ZOO!

Super Simple Preschool Practice • ©The Mailbox® Books • TEC61152

Note to the teacher: Use with "At the Zoo" on page 7.

_____

_____

_____

_____

_____

_____

Clothing Patterns

Use with "Coordinating Clothes" on page 13.

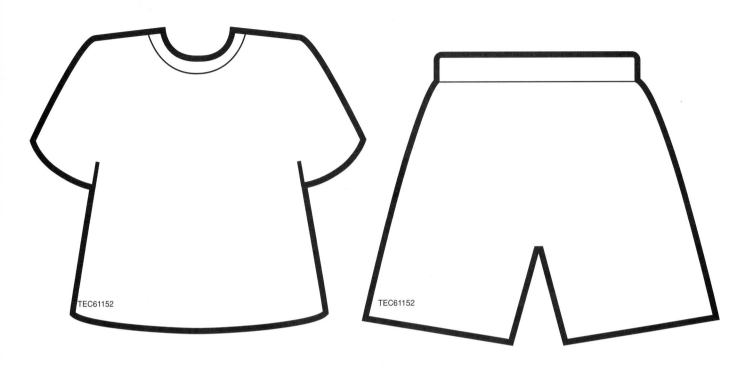

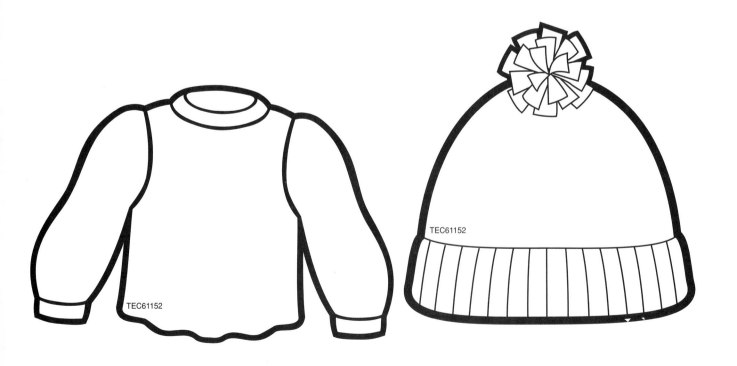

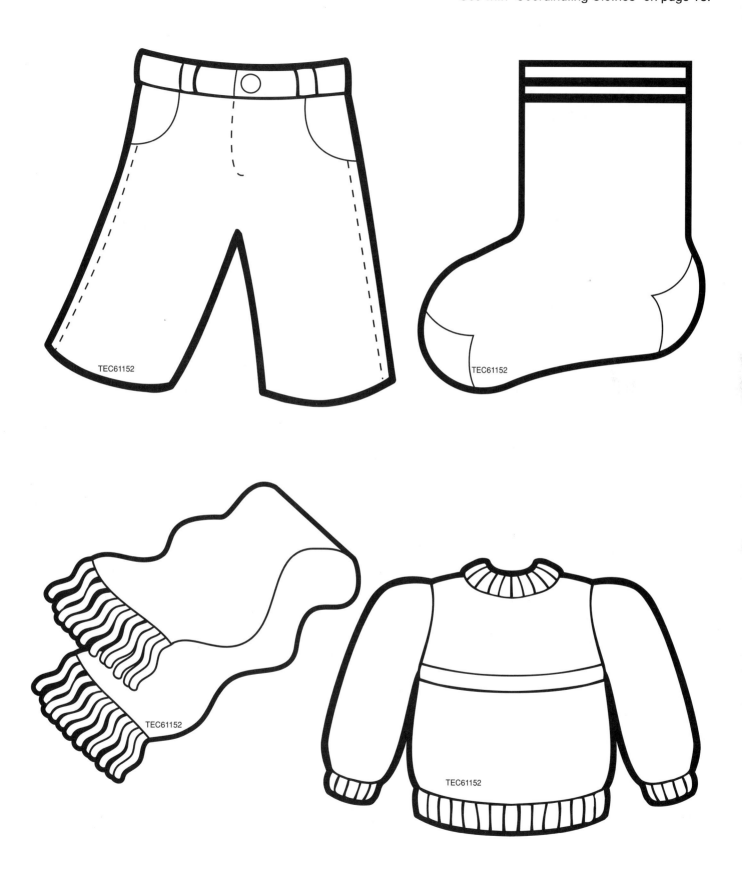

Rhyming Cards

Use with "Picture Patterns" on page 8 and "Picture Pairs" on page 16.

TEC61152

TEC61152

TEC61152

TEC61152

TEC61152

TEC61152

TEC61152

TEC61152

TEC61152

TEC61152

TEC61152

TEC61152

Doughnut Menu

$2.99 a dozen!

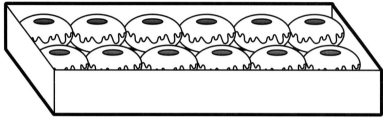

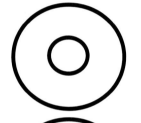 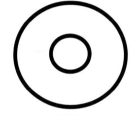 Chocolate

 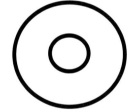 Jelly

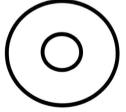 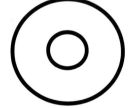 Cinnamon

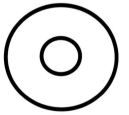 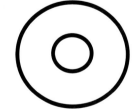 Blueberry

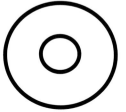 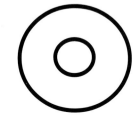 Glazed

Note to the teacher: Use with "Delicious Doughnuts" on page 17.

TEC61152

Car Cards

Use with "Milk Cap Match" on page 19.

Super Simple Preschool Practice • ©The Mailbox® Books • TEC61152

Road Sign Cards
Use with "So Many Signs" on page 21.

TEC61152

TEC61152

TEC61152

TEC61152

TEC61152

TEC61152

TEC61152

TEC61152

TEC61152

TEC61152

TEC61152

TEC61152

TEC61152

TEC61152

TEC61152

TEC61152

TEC61152

TEC61152

Gumball Machine Pattern
Use with "Gumballs Galore" on page 28.

TEC61152

Super Simple Preschool Practice • ©The Mailbox® Books • TEC61152

TEC61152
TEC61152
TEC61152
TEC61152
TEC61152
TEC61152
TEC61152
TEC61152

Dinosaur Bone Excavation Center

Super Simple Preschool Practice • ©The Mailbox® Books • TEC61152

Note to the teacher: Use with "Dino Dig" on page 31.

Peacock Pattern
Use with "Peculiar Peacock" on page 32.

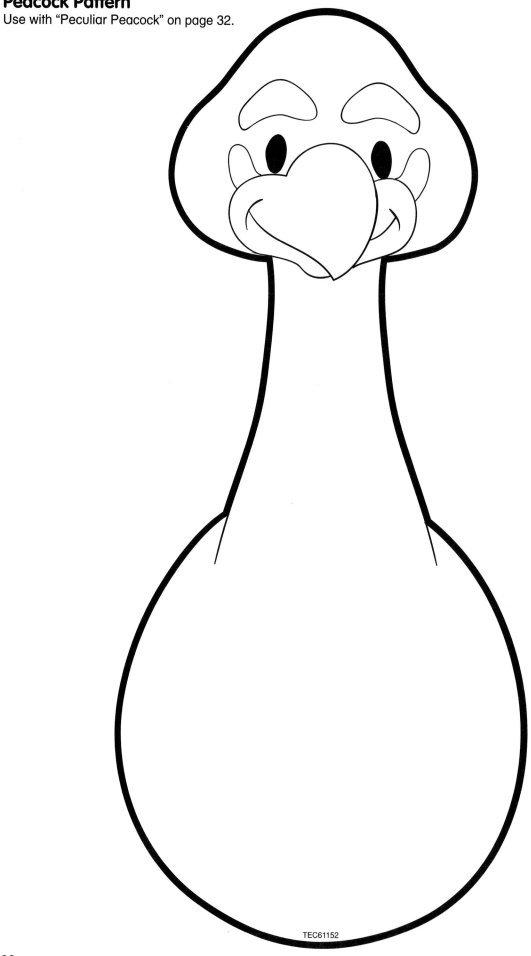

TEC61152

TEC61152

Beginning Sound Cards
Use with "Pig in a Puddle" on page 34.

TEC61152

TEC61152

TEC61152

TEC61152

TEC61152

TEC61152

TEC61152

TEC61152

Super Simple Preschool Practice • ©The Mailbox® Books • TEC61152

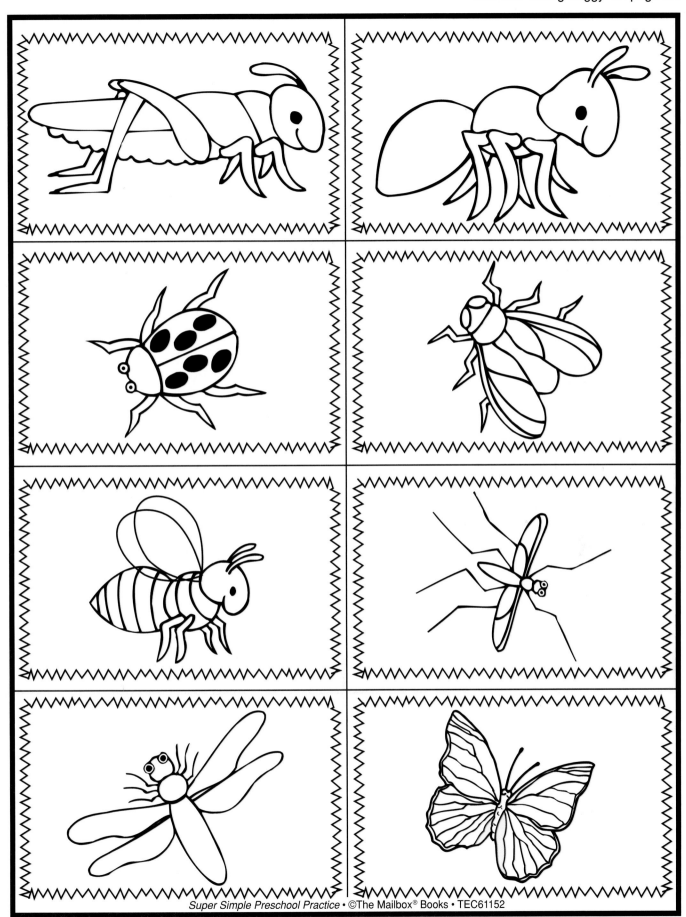

Super Simple Preschool Practice • ©The Mailbox® Books • TEC61152

Bug Cards

Use with "Going Buggy" on page 37.

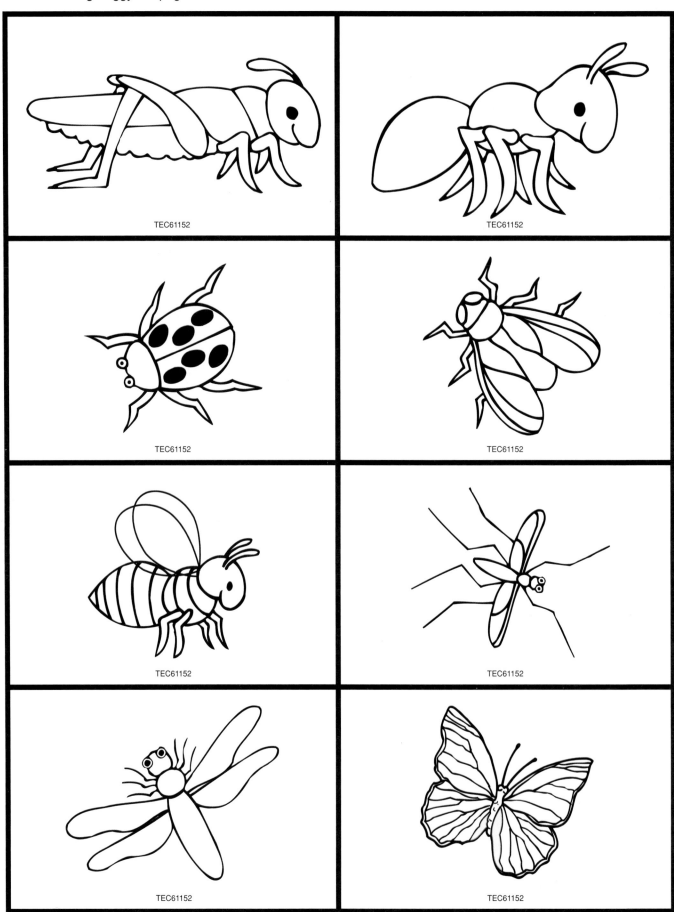

TEC61152

TEC61152

TEC61152

TEC61152

TEC61152

TEC61152

TEC61152

TEC61152

Super Simple Preschool Practice • ©The Mailbox® Books • TEC61152

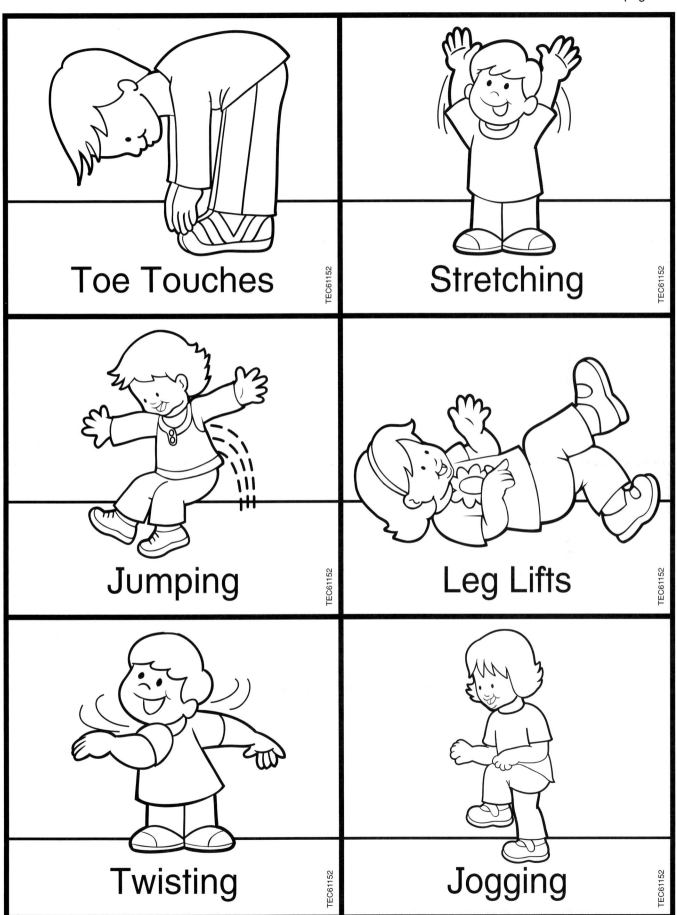

Toe Touches

TEC61152

Stretching

TEC61152

Jumping

TEC61152

Leg Lifts

TEC61152

Twisting

TEC61152

Jogging

TEC61152

Beginning Sound Cards

Use with "Time to Eat" on page 41.

TEC61152

TEC61152

TEC61152

TEC61152

TEC61152

TEC61152

TEC61152

TEC61152

TEC61152

TEC61152

TEC61152

TEC61152

TEC61152

TEC61152

TEC61152

TEC61152

Cow Pattern

Use with "Spotted Cow" on page 46.

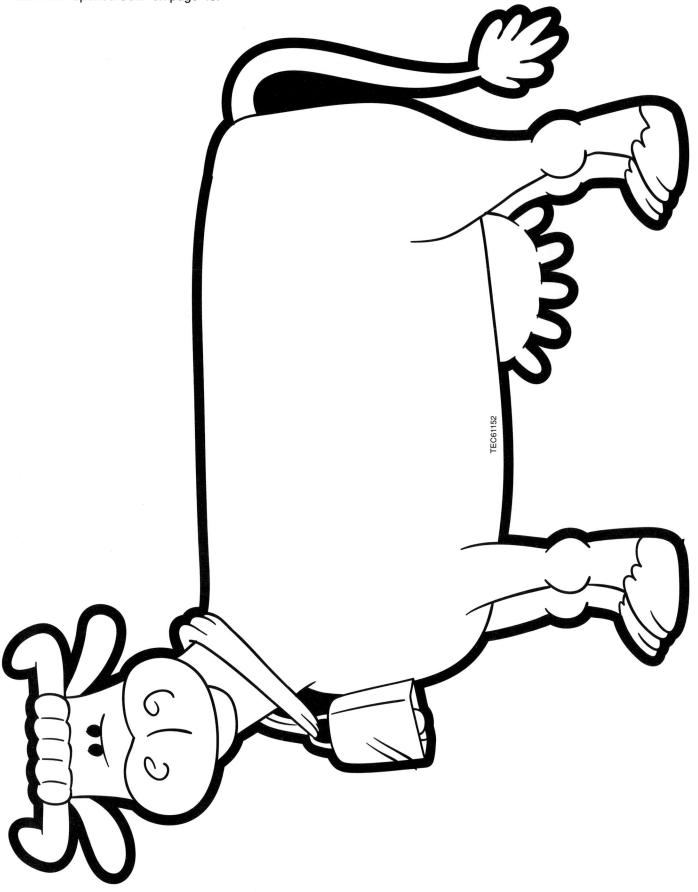

TEC61152

Super Simple Preschool Practice • ©The Mailbox® Books • TEC61152

Welcome to the
Preschool Pet Hospital

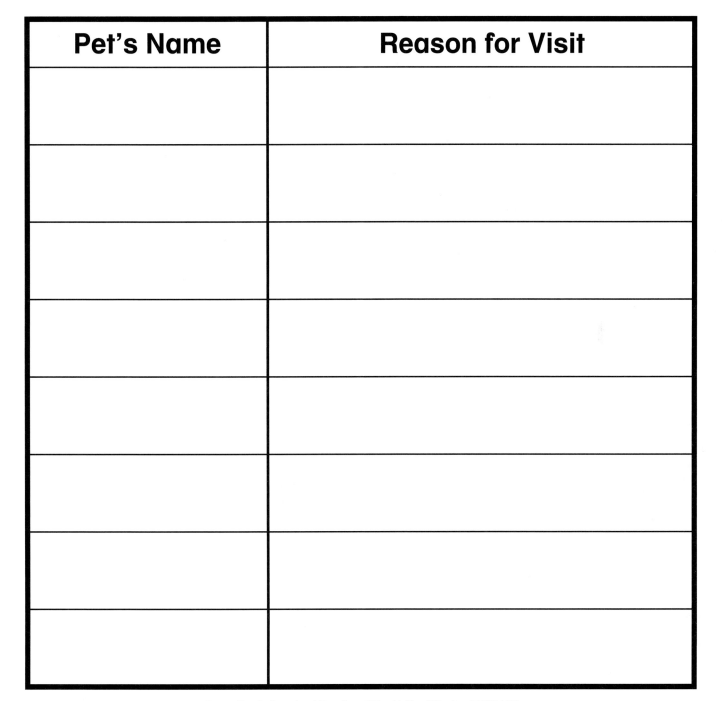

Pet's Name	Reason for Visit

Beginning Sound Cards

Use with "Searching for /s/" on page 50.

TEC61152

TEC61152

TEC61152

TEC61152

Crown Pattern
Use with "Royal Crowns" on page 51.

TEC61152

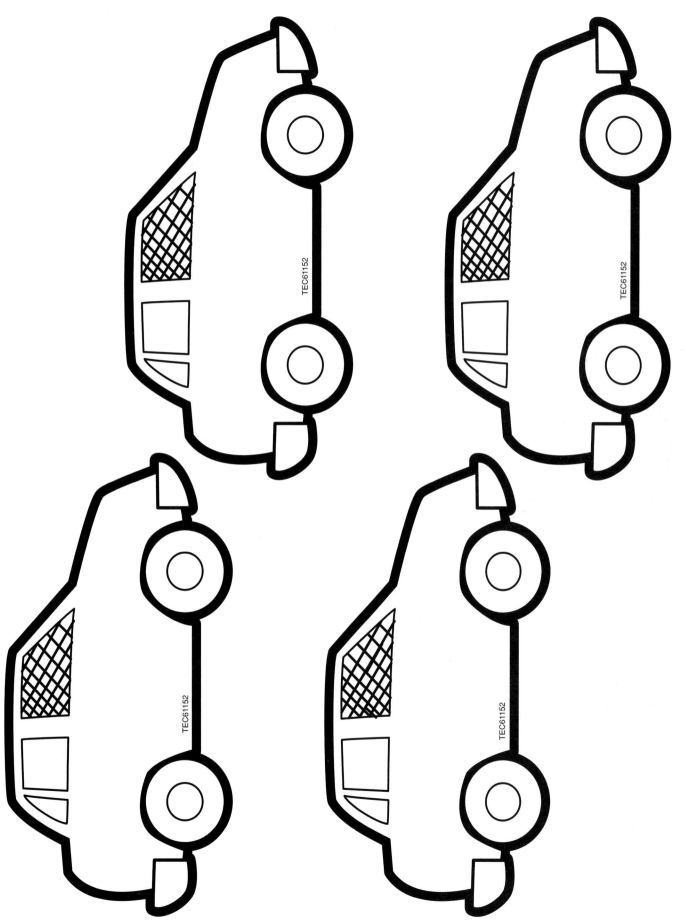

Fly Cards
Use with "Swat That Fly!" on page 61.

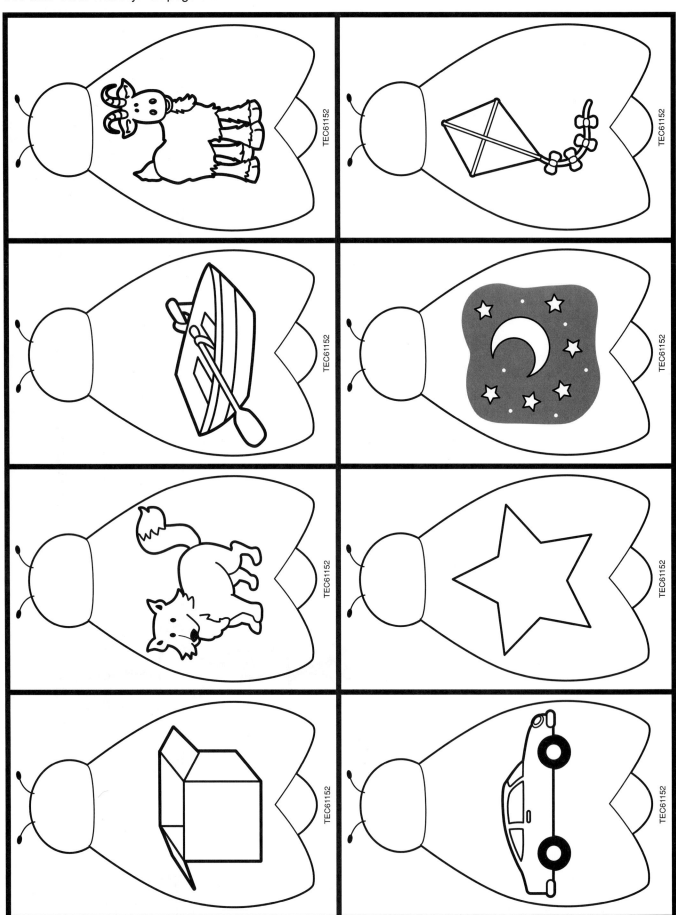

Super Simple Preschool Practice • ©The Mailbox® Books • TEC61152

TEC61152

TEC61152

TEC61152

TEC61152

Dog Pattern
Use with "Spot the Dog" on page 65.

TEC61152